A Red Room Basement

Rebellion Production

WHERE THE GRASSES WEPT

A COLLECTION OF POETRY

CHRISTOPHER RAINE

Preface

The most difficult thing about writing a book is holding the strands of your life together while you are doing it.

Real passion has a lot to do with suffering and sacrifice. You bare your soul, you put it out there on an aluminum dissection tray; a vivisection spread open and left on display.

People may like it, hate it, or ignore it. It's you, unapologetically.

Christopher Raine 2019/04/11

Also by Christopher Raine:

VACANT MORALITY: Poems of the Past
ISBN 978-1-4834-7808-1

CONTENTS

Chapter IV: Escapes

Chapter V: Love, Hate, and Indifference

Chapter VI: The Human Animal

Chapter VII: Endings and Farewells

Chapter VIII: Fais Ton Nom

About the Author

Acknowledgements

I would like to acknowledge the unwavering support of Stephen Dafoe of the Morinville News, the Morinville Community Public Library, and fellow poet, Jerry Skowronski. Of course, I could not forget the support of my beloved wife whom, despite my protests, has suffered with me for a great many years.

Chapter I:
Once Upon a Time

BACK EAST

BACK EAST

I dream of

the smallest of strawberries

with white petal flowers

plush blackberry swaths

of green bushes

spider webs among oak leaves

and acorns

autumn mornings

and damp leaves

stones thick with moss

and mushrooms

blue-spotted salamanders

and the scent of black earth

the cool mist

of a salt-ocean breeze

dragonflies as big as your hand

the delicious smoke

of faded grey shacks

filled with mackerel

the smile of a fisherman's face

the price of a good deal

the glint of a glass

and the sweet-amber fragrance

2

of a navy spiced rum

I dream of a home

lost along the way

of things

that used to be

SACRIFICE OF A SINGLE MOTHER

SACRIFICE OF A SINGLE MOTHER

I remember the first time
I tied my own shoe laces
sitting on the wooden stairs
that fell into the basement
a moment of pride
I wanted to show someone
that I could do it
I was a big boy now,
but my father was gone
and my mother worked
at the hair salon
so there was nobody there
to share it with

My mother,
in whose arms I felt love
and a kind of sadness;
without her there was silence
she would have been there
if she could have
I am certain that she would have
I can imagine her there
marvelling at the

4

intricacy of the knot

these tiny hands made

there on the steps

in that tiny home

with the oak trees

and the strawberries

that grew in the field

I think of my mother now

three thousand miles away

getting older

getting frailer

I stand in wonder

of everything she's done

of how her heart was never

too small to love

the smallest things

the sacrifices she made;

to work and to provide

while she missed out

on the greatest

and smallest

of wonders

A PENNY

When I was ten

maybe eleven

we'd catch frogs from the culvert

at the edge of town

by the railway tracks

I can still hear

the washboard sway of barley fields

and the grinding-chattering

of grasshoppers in our ears

Carly is here too

with his blond hair

his perpetually red-chapped lips

and green eyes

here we are

wading in stagnant water

beside swaths of cattails

poking out from the earth

like corn dogs at a fair

I smell earthy peat and sour water

mixed with the satisfying

industrial scent of dirty oil and metal

if we had any change

after Popeye Cigarettes

and wads of fat chewing gum

we'd put pennies on the rails

and wait for the next train

hiding in barley like snipers

we'd watch and wait

you can feel that train coming

even long out of sight

a fleshy palm on the iron rail

would tell you

long before you could see it

that's when the pennies go down;

when we'd take our positions in the field

the train would come

the rails shaking

the engineer blasting his horn

the snorting bull of a territorial charge!

we'd wait

through clacking-heavy thunder!

we'd wait until it passed

before collecting our flattened treasures

it isn't all that easy

to get that kind of thrill for a penny

in fact they don't even

make them

anymore

PEANUT BUTTER

I opened up a jar of peanut butter

with the safety-seal still intact

pulling back that foil-paper-plastic tab

the scent of peanuts caught my nose

it's funny how elephants eat peanuts

they say that they have great memories

I wouldn't know, I'm neither scientist

nor pachyderm, but sometimes I remember

I was in a Dartmouth suburb

one might argue that all of Dartmouth

is a suburb, maybe even the whole province

I might have been three or four

early childhood stuff

the stuff that clings to the fringes and folds

of your mind like peanut butter

to the roof of your mouth

like your first jack-in-the-box

that weird poking music it made before

that clown face jumps out at you

those memories stick

now I'm driving a battery powered car

it was red, might have been modelled

after a corvette but it's too blurry to tell

in the myopic lens of the mind

the driveway was packed dirt

maybe gravel

but those little hollow-plastic wheels

scratched the pebbles and drove me forward

just the same, mostly in circles

I remember my mother calling my name

is it funny that I can't remember her voice?

she stood at the top of the dull

blue painted wooden steps

at the screen door smoothing her skirt

I don't want to come in

but it's lunch time

that strikes me as funny

'lunchtime'

from a child's perspective

it's all so different

somehow during my 9-5 day job

as a toddler

I'd have to break for lunch

at the appointed hunger-less time

I went inside and stuffed peanut butter

sandwiches with thick rough bread

into my face and cheeks

like a goddamn machine

it wasn't pre-sliced bread;

it was sawn like a log
or a side of beef
the peanut butter was thick
on dry bread,
but with cold milk it was magic
after hurried eating
I went back outside
with sticky fingers and a milk moustache
I saw other kids running away
one kid in particular
was four or five years older
than me; a giant more or less
it's all about perspective
age is forever when you're young
so that fat little bastard,
back in the days when you
never saw fat kids,
decided to test drive
a toddler's tiny electric car
he broke the axel
and cracked the plastic body
nearly in half
then ran away laughing
my mom knew the kid
and his alcoholic old man
with his greasy boat-mechanic hands

and unwashed breath
not much a single mom could do,
not in those days,
against a man like that
she'd have been asking for trouble
sure as hell couldn't buy another one
I think she cursed at them
it was too late for it
she couldn't console her crying
little boy either
but she tried
I screwed the plastic lid
back onto the jar of peanut butter
and put it back in the pantry
closing the folding white door behind

I miss my mother
and the peanut butter?
I guess I just wasn't craving it
after all

I REMEMBER NANA

I remember my Nana

gasping on the floor

her glasses pressed

awkwardly against her face

a thin wisp of spittle

ran from her frozen mouth

while ragged air rasped

in gurgles from her lungs

I was nine, maybe ten

I remember the doctor

who told her to exercise

and to eat less salt

I remember Nana

walking from the porch

to the front sidewalk;

exhausted and miserable

I remember when

her feet caught on fire

while warming them

with the space heater

but mostly

I remember her terrified eyes

blue and grey

12

and a little cruel

I saw tears in them

while I held her hand

and waited for the ambulance

they said I was brave

that I did good

I remember feeling helpless

and that I felt shame

because I knew deep down

that I wasn't brave at all

L'AÉROPORTS DE MONTRÉAL

L'AÉROPORTS DE MONTRÉAL

Staring out of windows

at L'Aéroports de Montréal

snow skiffs across the tarmac

a grey fog paints the sky

distances recede into obscurity

carpet tiles are frayed and lifting

I hear a vacuum sucking

whining in that high-pitched

mechanical scream

as a maintenance worker labours

you can feel the sound in your teeth

the rattle of debris chiming

through the ribbed hose

I've got hours to kill

not enough for a meaningful venture

beyond this stale prison

I overhear a business conversation

from a stranger's cell phone

louder and more clearly

than muffled airport announcements

outside smeared windows

a turboprop sits at gate two

time is relative

time can be unwanted and slow

time can heal wounds

I remember that an old love of mine

lives here in Montréal

somewhere I don't know exactly,

after all it's been thirty six years

I knew then

as a boy of some fifteen years

that I was in love

and that I loved her

with everything I had

everything I was

and when she left,

she told me

with the sage wisdom

of a few months

that I did not understand love

that it was infatuation

nothing more

as we waited for the plane

that would take her from me

we hugged and kissed

and cried together for the last time

now here I am

so far from that moment

staring out from the window of the airport

that once brought you to me

I look at the unmoving-grey stillness

where the dull sky meets pale ice

and February snow

I long to know;

where you are now?

how your life turned out?

I wanted to tell you

that you were wrong

Chapter II:
Natural Love

DULCINEA

Can you see me in your sunlight
reflected by the sea
where time is crystal amber
or frozen, somewhere in-between?

Will you ponder for just a moment
when you think of you and me
of the friends and the old neighbours
and other things you used to see?

Can you feel from that penthouse
the texture of your dreams
the colours and the flavours
and the places you have been?

Succoured in a mirrored palace
the windows reflect what they've seen
from the shadows and open curtains
to the open spaces of your means

I'd love to be your knight in armour
or something like that old theme
I've never been that much for romance
but it's all that's left of me

If you should fall from your tower
a broken doll with broken schemes
you'll find me down here waiting
or somewhere, where I dream

SURRENDER

She revealed to me
her forbidden love
in sight yet out of reach
a fragrant flower so divine
the nectar warm and sweet
the knowledge of its presence
unfolded in the heat
the breath of life within me fell
as wisdom sinking to defeat
I beg before this beauty
I worship at her feet
I surrender to this longing
my defences in retreat
I offer up my broken-love,
it's tired but it's still sweet
and though I will never
know her touch at all
I long for its relief

PURPLE OCEAN

If we were to be somewhere
where we could suppose
some other place
to sit among desires
that were dreamt
and not misplaced
to bathe
in orange moonlight
beside a purple ocean scape
to know our own desires
and each other's
in embrace
in this love
a deeper being
than any I could state
in warm eyes
that always smile
with tenderness and grace
to suppose
some other somewhere
in the sands our fingers traced
our breathless names
beside this ocean
this eternal sacred space

AT ANY MOMENT

At any moment

at any second

at any passing of the day

I'll take the time

just to say

what you mean to me

When you're tired

and you're wondering

how you will ever

make it through?

hold on tight, take this love

it was once a part of me

In the evening

while the moon cries

and you're watching your TV

have a drink

put your feet up

that's okay with me

No, I don't need you

but I want you

please don't change
there is no need
as you are, that is all
that it needs to be

We can dance
beneath the dust
beside the dishes in the sink
I don't mind, it's alright
you are the only thing
I'm going to see

There are problems
there are pressures
baby, they don't
mean a thing
when we kiss, when we cry
it's just a memory

At any moment
at any second
while our life just fades away
I'll take the time
I'll take your hand
that's all love means to me

DRINKING IN THE MOONLIGHT

I'll be drinking in the moonlight
after a glass or after a few
the distant stars in all of heaven
our eyes, the mirrors to all we view

There may be no god above us
no more judgements, no last reviews
our ashes and our possessions
the last remains of me and you

There can be no greater meaning
if I could share this life in truth
all of my being, all of my knowing
I would share it all with you

Won't you join me in the moonlight
after a glass or after a few?
honour me for just a moment
my only one I'd give to you

GHOSTS

I've been haunting
fading memories
those distant times
still linger there
for me to see
the well-travelled path
that led
from you to me

Can I claim
that it was meant to be?
ghosts in the mist
they whisper
so seductively
their moistened breath
refreshing
as a newborn sea

If you weren't here
I know that I
would rather be
anywhere or anyplace
I could no longer see

among the dying
and the departed
lost parts of me

A world without love
or sympathy
no compassion
no care and no empathy
this is the place
I would choose to be
if I could not have you here
along with me

DESIDERATUM

There's a chair there, beside the change room
it looks just like an ancient heirloom
but it gives me some small respite of release
the taupe carpet here is comforting
the muzak, sterile and unthreatening
the vinyl tiles, provide a pattern to relief

As I sit there amongst the racket
like a tired old man in a smoking jacket
an ill-fit toupee and a half-filled cognac dream
I am reminded of Alfred Prufrock's parlor life
though he never lived to a have wife
never a wife nor any other precious scheme

From the secrets of the change rooms
women come and go with their glooms
gasping in frustration for what does or doesn't show
but the mannequins are absolute perfection
smooth and perfect in their erection
like the statues of the great Michelangelo

While the hangers clang in rattled protest
as they scrape both to and fro in behest

to the whims and wiles of scarlet letter dreams

there are no more fitted garments

"One fits none!" they cry and lament

they weep for imperfections fit for none

I WANT

I want to write a poem about love
to write a smile on your face
to pen your laughter on the page

I want to paint your skin
in sunlight-sienna tan lines
flavoured with tropical scented oils

I want you in autumn walks
coloured leaves and morning chills
coffee houses and ginger snaps

I want to feel your warm body
beside a crackling fireplace
snuggled under a blanket

I want an end to the frozen chill
of winter Douglas firs
in collars of wet virgin snow

I want you to melt this glacial heart
to expose the black fertile earth
to renew our growing love again

LINES WITH EYELASHES

My wife is flailing her arms

flipping her fingers

frantically emphasizing expressions

and I'm just saying

"Baby, I didn't take no goddamn

sign language pill!"

she laughs then smiles

with a waxing gibbous grin

the kind that delights a room;

her eyes mere-squinting lines

with eyelashes

God, I love her laugh

and the way she brings me down

just enough to keep me humble

she keeps me real

as any real thing can be

concrete and firm

she'd hate me saying, "concrete"

like the way she believes herself to be

inferior somehow,

but let me tell you

she's the better part of wisdom

while I'm just smoking in the clouds

WE LAUGH

Yeah, we're going broke

wages going down

costs going up

we find our laughter

under seat cushions

like loose change

amongst the crumbs

my wife and I

leaning on each other

like two playing cards

waiting for a gust of wind

to knock us down

I make her a piña colada

I drink my rum with ice

when it's good

with cola when it's not

I'm almost out of cola now

we listen to music

and bitch about life

then we laugh

we laugh

in gallows mirth

giddy and morose

we lie in a bed

of satire and dead flowers

in barren gardens

as autumn falls

we laugh

MARRIED TO DEATH

I'm married to death
or so it would seem
she's grown tired of life
grown tired of the scene
she's fucked, but she's funny
can't do better than that
she ain't tall, she ain't skinny
you wouldn't say she was fat
she laughs when she's lonely
she cries when she's mean
she's the life of the party
and the first one to leave
all of these things
my love tends to be
a ragged old mess
but still better than me

WHITE KITTEN

an electric fan

patters a chopped breeze

a white river of sound

drowning and numb

"Some people like it"

she says

'Others do not.'

a silent retort echoes

'It's just noise

no matter what

colour you call it'

annoyance flutters

at the edge of the mind

a pale moth in moonlight

he arranges his pillow

again and again

a fat man kneading dough

he sighs dropping his head

a stone weight

held on a candy string

of popping ligaments

and tenuous tendons

his wife sleeps there

beside him

her inky hair spilled

across the pillow

like an erotic dream

It comes easily to her;

the sleep

she snores softly

cat-like

it's almost a comfort to hear

but after a while

it's just noise

TOGETHER

He sat in the living room
The television was on
it had been there
chattering away
flickering light and shadow;
a storm
blinding light and sound
watch me!
worship me!
need me!
drunk from idle divinity
the man sat
quietly in the corner
smoking of potential
oblivious and lost
to the squall of flat worlds
transcendent and distant
his wife sat in another room
they were both
in the same place
and in no place
together

WORN OLD WALLET

I found a photo of you in my old wallet
when I was cleaning up the place
it was tucked in behind the torn plaid liner
a faded smile upon your face

On the back you had written a little something
a tender promise so naive and so very sweet
your girlish cursive smeared across the paper
worn out by time, the leather, and the heat

I held it in my hands for a while
it was forgotten there for years
I remembered you fondly in that moment
we were in love or so it appeared

But we never should have been together
we were incompatible and so poorly cast
we never considered what could divide us
we never knew tomorrow could be the past

And there you were in my dresser
beside the watch with a broken clasp
another sign, a symbol of the meaning
we now know forever never lasts

CROSSINGS
CROSSINGS

Colours brighten

in the eyes of the dying

the distances narrow

the rivers are drying

a bridge crosses still

from the place where it drew

the love and the hate,

the old places we knew

old anger so distant

you forgot what it means

the torrents of passion

are no more than streams

there are no crossings needed

after the waters have passed

as the distance between us

drys in days long since past

Chapter III:
Fate of Nations

A MAN WHO BEGS FOR FLEAS

We are all up for crucifixion
there's no willing
just desperate pleas
and some living long for dying,
but there's no proof in mysteries

A crucifix stabbed into heaven
on that dusty hill
at Calvary
left forsaken in his suffering
some fathers are hard to please

A muddle of strangled delusion
in a world that was never
meant for ease
acquisitions and endless treasures;
a homeless man who begs for fleas

For an ending free of suffering
we've all been aching
just to be
to love in a loveless world
that whispers divinity to me

BOTTLED

Bottles of plastic water
lie upon your grocer's shelf
choose whichever one you want
that's freedom, you tell yourself
The choices here don't matter,
not the ones that you've been told
if they did, you'd never have them
that's the deal you've been sold

You feel safe behind that label
of colour and baseless claim
your brands are neatly separated
but they're really all the same
Faced neatly in the line up
and so precisely contained
behind those labelled blindfolds
the heraldry and the shame

They'll dump you on the street
after their thirst has been quenched
when you're drained and fully empty
and the best parts of you are spent
They will make a brand new product

out of what they've ground from you

and fill it with the same tap water

that all of them still use

It will have a brand new label

it's pure and it's improved!

it's the same damn vessel of liquid

but at least you get to choose

FLOWERS AT THE MARKET

There are flowers at the market
they are bleeding there in view
a bloodletting in expression of
the sweet fragility of me and you

There's a rose between your teeth
and a white lily beside a cross
a lotus flower upon an altar
and fresh cut sorrows for the lost

A carnation for your man's lapel
the tulips of the nuptial bouquet
a dabble of sympathetic magic
to keep restless spirits at bay

I suppose it is only fitting
when one considers this abuse
our sensual dance of sex and death
fragrant euphemisms for this truth

A THEIST

I am an atheist who seeks divinity
that's not found within a trinity
you might say a curious affinity
but I will need more evidence to decide

An examination of obscurity
a hope for simple purity
an answer without a mystery
for something we're unable to define

But I want an end to suffering
an end to mindless mutterings
and the ceaseless tribal butchering
that's been marching through all time

So until we can define it
I'm content to just deny it
I'll need evidence to describe it
that's not something I am willing to concede

I'm not interested in vague opinion
or the rote of some dominion
or the fracture of a tired schism
your ancestors struggled to describe

But I believe in all our science
and in its use and its appliance
I'll stand here in plain defiance
until the facts are there for us to see

But I am certainly uncertain
of any man behind the curtain
and so I must once again refrain
to knowledge that lies beyond this doubt

Because sadly I've seen so little
no proof beyond acquittal
still no answer to the riddle
I know it's something we haven't seen before

EIGHTEEN DOLLARS

The country music scratches
over the metal intercom speaker;
an irritating itch
the sterile-white fluorescent tubes
make love to the stained ceiling tiles
while the Formica outpatient desk
speaks volumes of redundant lore
laminated paper information
tacky-tape tinged
browned at the edges
like dirty old bandages
unthreatening clip art
and poor font choices
not enough information
to keep this charred mind burning
I paid for two hours of parking
I'm told I might be waiting four
I don't have another
nine dollars to spend
disability pensions are cruel
the greatest expenses are paid
by those who suffer the most
and have the least

LUCIFER'S COMPLAINT

You slipped behind your shadow
like the stone before the cave
you wear a skin of sweet submission
but you're the master, I'm the slave

How I've felt you in my longing
how I've shuddered from this heat
I've marvelled at your creation
you're above and I'm beneath

An adversary plain and simple
who never wore a thorny crown
who never made a sinner sin
who never let his people drown

But I'm in love with your illusion
how I'd like a little peace
there are demons all within us
some above and some beneath

PARKADE

Sleeping in the stairwell
of a damp cement parkade
crumpled in the corner
left vulnerable and afraid

It doesn't matter where you go,
what you do, or what you say
you're the pariah and the vermin
and that's your life today

As the people walk on by
they never look your way
they'll report you to the cops
you're unsightly where you stay

Oh, there once was a time
in a forgotten secret grace
mama held you in her arms
you were warmed by her embrace

But that's all just a dream
now distant and out of place
invisible and discarded
long lost without a trace

PAX AMERICANA

They could have
sung of love songs
or of a romance
by the sea
fields flush
with wild horses
or a love not
meant to be

They could have
sung of charity
or compassion
or of glee
a garden
of temptations
or some erotic
mystery

They could have
made the pax
and dreamt
of things to be
all citizens
of paradise

with no one
on their knees

They could have
fought off hunger
no more genocide
no more need
they could have
fought for freedom
but instead
they fought for thee

TREE UPON A HILL

A mother once prayed

beside an open solemn grave

but no one now

remembers her name

a young man lies there still

beneath that tree upon the hill

he's been lying there

since before you were born

did her aging womb decay

like the flowers that once rained

after the old men,

sent the young men to die?

the wooden cross in disarray

the letters lost and worn away

a family legacy now feeds

the mushrooms and the mites

the tears from a loving mother

salt and water like any other

another droplet

bleeds its way into the sea

in this misery we all dwell

and our children sent to hell

the crumbling martyrs

of our vanity and greed

broken brains and clotted blood

this end; a grieving mother's love

I swear it's more than any

living man can take

GROCERY CART

His back was slumped
up against the brick wall
of the pharmacy
beneath the iron bars
that covered windows
plastered with posters
for Tiger-balm and Pokémon

His aluminum can possessions
beside him there
in the garbage bags
immeasurable wealth secured
by the stolen grocery cart
with the untouchable
greasy plastic handle

Don Quixote and his trusty companion
what windmills they faced
in the feral streets
questing for his Lady Dulcinea
the princess who slept in the Toyota
and gave out hand jobs
for dumpster food tributes

REQUIEM FOR VENUS

Her clothes hung on her
like open boxes of guilt
pleasures of creation
starved in longing
to the congestion of confessions
and propriety enslaved
trivial matters of flesh and skin
guilt driven into the mind
stabbing like an icicle
of fear and shame
surrendering to the control
of sterile-white hands
the smell of old men
and parchment-thin paper

POSTCARD FROM YEMEN

curved lines

cage-clutched

and concave

claw at tiny lungs

a butterfly heart pounds

anemic pulses

of undernourished

oil-stained blood

glassy brown eyes

stare through eternity

while the hollow wind

cries to a plain

of dust scattered souls

and broken cinderblocks

a desperate mother

milks sand

from the casings

of brass tears

in an improvised manger

of torn plastic rags

a star in the east

calls to the magi

that never

come to call

THE BEACH

Waves of heavy grass
brushed against fingertips
and salty seaweed
dried dark and crisp
carelessly swept
across warm sand
crunching like celluloid
beneath sandaled feet
ticker tape from a quietly
deserted street;
a parade long ended
the disappointed
return to their homes alone.
my god, you can almost hear
the brass band
and widowed women weeping
beneath the silence of the wind
while the ocean,
dedicated and devoted,
keeps time with its
inexorable caress
coloured towels
draw lines in the shore
defining families like nations

castles in the sand
rise and fall
while children stutter in protest
"Mama, I'm not cold!"
all the while
betrayed by blue lips
and shaking shivers

SONG OF THE SIREN

SONG OF THE SIREN

While the choir sings softly
with a hymn that is sweet
and a beauty that slips
through the soul
its praise and its glory
so far beyond worry
you offer lucre
to the heavenly shoals

Where they sing and they dance
to the idle romance
and the notion of something so pure
a jest has been made
by the men in brocades
the mitres and vestments allure

They'll guide your soul for a while
if you don't ever smile
and tithe all the earnings you make
admission is paid
for the sins that you made
and the cherubs are all on the take

Aye, the Lord is a miser

you've thought none the wiser

for the crumbs and the wine

that you drank

it's expensive enough

and you all share a cup

and then bow your head in thanks

While the choir sings softly

with a hymn that is sweet

and a beauty that slips

through the soul

its praise and its glory

so far beyond worry

you offer lucre

to the heavenly shoals

WILFRED OWEN

It's cold down in the trenches
where the men line up like cattle
"Keep your head down! My brother,
when the machine guns start to rattle."

There was once a splendid meadow
wild flowers grew upon the way
a school house in the distance
you could hear the children play

The fields are wound in barbed wire
and the land is slick with blood
there's no comfort in the hell below
but it's safer than above

The mustard gas comes crawling,
the ragged breath of a homeless man
the burning and gargled screaming
get your masks on if you can.

The scream of the mortars falling
like the banshee of Celtic lore
aye, that harbinger of death
has come knocking at your door

Wilfred Owen in the Great War
with the rats as thick as cats
one week before it was ended
he became a poet of the past

Another hole there, in the cemetery
in Ors of Northern France
another grave, another soldier
another poet without romance

There's no glory for the dying
there's no hurrah to victory
there's just the casualty of seeing
what no man should ever see

He saw war for what it was
there was no good reason for the call
not for king and not for country
there is no point to it at all.

MYSTERY

I have looked and I have looked
but I couldn't find the light
so I cried out to the darkness
until the darkness became delight

I am parched by the unknowing
and I just may be accursed
I may not have the answers, but
there are many fates much worse

Leave me dying in this desert
leave me dying of this thirst
leave me to seek forbidden fruit
for I will never be coerced

And though my throat is parched
I won't drink from His hammered cup
the grail is not for knowing
it is for those who've given up

So I will seek out every wisdom
to reveal all there is to show
I am infinite in my ignorance
I long for all there is to know

REPUBLIC

If you recall all the reckoning
that was wreaked upon rest
the tired and the poor
the clothed and the undressed
the tiny little picture
in your wallet in the drawer
the passport for the guilt
we keep on distant shores

All the suffering of suffragettes
the seditious screaming roar
the neutering of homosexuals
wanting love and nothing more
the prisoners of forbidden sex
begging on their knees
all for the democratic chore
so neglected by the free

Left alone to your devices
favorite apps and favourite screens
a blanket of smothering confirmation
while what's real is left unseen
all that matters is the matter

take the time and stake a claim

lest tyranny raise its trembling fist

with ourselves the ones to blame

Chapter IV:
Escapes

DASHBOARD VINYL

DASHBOARD VINYL

Our exhaust

trailed behind us

black pavement drawing

grease pencil lines

on smooth butcher paper

while shimmering air danced

making love to the horizon

the scent of dashboard vinyl

played like an old record

in the passenger seat she smiled

her hair restrained beneath a silk scarf

eyes hidden beneath dark glasses

the wind buffets at that speed

making conversation impossible

but it didn't matter; we didn't need any

ahead blue skies kissed the clouds

while the sun god laughed

tomorrow was always ahead

yesterday in the rear view mirror

and the in-between

a distant memory

CATS DIG IT

Her legs were like the Sudan

smooth and endless

reaching out to forever

I can still feel

the shimmering heat

of that little black dress she wore

the kind of one every woman

is supposed to have

that slid across her desert

like a cool long shadow

a drink of shade

to a sweating heart

when she spoke

it was as if you were drinking

your own soul

smooth as a morning lake

on a windless day

or a cool mist that

lingers like smoke from

a jazz players lips

take a second to just

breathe that in

She takes to the stage
with a subtle sway
the kind that makes
a grown man's mouth cry
a hush falls
like the captured whisper
of a stolen secret
the band strikes in
first a sweet brushed hi-hat
and tight snare to match
followed by snapping fingers
flickering in that cool, sweet bliss
the lights come up on that
sublimely statuesque neck
and shadowed jaw line
leaving you begging
for her tulip mouth to open
with that supple siren's song;
a voice that brought
the goddamn Argonauts
to their knees
And then it begins

NOVEMBER STILL

I was up early this morning
before the breaking of the day
I could not sleep another moment
I could not dream my life away

So I brewed myself a coffee
and I smoked a little weed
I was contented by the silence
it was a moment without a need

It was early in November
and the snow began to fall
I could almost clearly hear it
winter spirits and their call

I am complacent in contentment
in this world silent and still
you can strain but never hear it;
a prophet aching for god's will

And maybe it was in that moment
that I found my sacred place
it was just outside the world
in the stillness I found the grace

SELENE

And where are you? Oh, distant light
that came in wonder now out of sight
behind the clouds and so far out of reach
I saw you sighing in the sky above
from darkness, light, this goddess love
a glowing siren calling out to me

So many names, my dear Selene,
Artemis, Hecate, and Phoebe
inspired beauty of those pagan dreams
you are maiden, mother, and the crone
you walk the night, but you're not alone
the stars in heaven, a backdrop to your scene

The clouds collapse, they came and went
they fondled you and have been spent
but you shine on in lasting purity
the winter wolves still howl for you
the frozen pines in silhouette view,
the snow covered hills bathing in your sheen

NIRVANA IN SUMMER

The feeling of indifference

licks the city haze

stinking of diesel fuel

and groping filthy fingers

the road dreams of tar

and brake dust

but the wind caresses

while the top is down

with the lustful touch

of an easy lover

the road rubs

against the rubber

moaning and droning

the blissful hum

of distance and speed

leaving the city behind

for the open road

get away!

anywhere but here

there is no distance

far enough!

no space

big enough!

the illusion of freedom
sweet and intoxicating;
to drive off of the edge
of nirvana in summer

STILLNESS OF THE MORN

STILLNESS OF THE MORN

In the stillness of the morn
in the pause between each breath
in that moment of perfect silence
between your life and death

The clarity it comes to you
like a servant at your door
when there is nothing left of you,
there can be no longing anymore

The fleeting and the eternal
both the silence and the roar
the calm before the fury
and the spaces between doors

A moment in that passage
like some lost forgotten lore
a tinkling through the hourglass
in the sands of the obscure

A release into your wisdom
with no attachments anymore
the ravens of that Norse god
who both whisper 'nevermore'

Let it all fall away from you
until you can feel it no more
a moment of silent freedom
in the stillness of the morn

STRANGER

The stranger in the sunlight
cast a shadow from far away
an eclipse in the making
the man who would not stay

A guitar slung over his shoulder
a host of songs for him to play
long nails on his strumming fingers
thinning hair half turned to grey

He will sing a lonely ballad
to empty halls and empty days
his voice rumbles deep in timbre
his soul-filled eyes are far away

He will tell you the same old story
the one he's told most every day
about lost love and lingering sadness;
careless places, forgotten strays

There's another lonely woman
and she's single for the day
she invites the stranger to her bed
for some other kind of play

While her heart is full and open
to the romance that he played
middle age felt a little further
from the burden of her days

The stranger in the sunlight
cast a shadow from far away
an eclipse in the making
the man who would not stay

THE ANGEL'S SHARE

Taken over time

the innocence we wept

evaporates

whispered breaths

upon the wind

droplets of spoken words

condensate

upon cataract panes

overlooking the streets

of bedroom strangers

and one night cheap hotels

the barmaid smiles

and leans toward you

pressing a sweaty glass

into your dry shaking hand

"Drink," she whispers

in a smoky voice

that scratches the

hidden spaces

of your warmest itch

"to life,"

she tilts her own glass

of clinking ice and bitters,

"it is all that remains

after the angels have taken

their share."

WHERE THE GRASSES WEPT

There was a moment
straining out of view
beside a window wet with pain
another second
where the grasses wept
amongst the fields of the plain

A glimpse of smiling sunshine
that laughed
then winked away
distant thunder sadly grumbles
like the voices
that once played

Crying out to the sky above
like seagulls
when they complain
I'd like to walk
amongst the sunshine
in those fields of yesterday

I long for that brilliant light
that breaks on

through the grey

but the moment

that came and went

has since been washed away

If you can weather

out the storm

with a heart made out of clay

come and find me

in those faded places

long lost to yesterday

JOSEPH OF ARIMATHEA

Feeling the breeze through

a half-open kitchen window

rum and coke in my hand

ice sparkles in caramel gold

the cola fizz pops

a battered barstool

wearing a cheap suit

hangs like torn rags

over the Pillars of Heracles

I'd cry if I still could

I laugh because I can't

feeling numb

and morosely self-aware

a taunting recognition

of hope glimmers

another glass

of reality shimmers

whispering beneath the shade

of an old lamp

lingering laugh lines

dreaming the sweet smile

of a summer lake

a hallowed loon clears

the yielding morning reeds

a drop of gold weeps

as the sun melts the waters

THE PRIVATEER

The air falls out of his heavy lungs
sails flagging to a gasping breeze
declining in all of his measure and wit
succumbing to his peculiar disease
a carrack destined to run aground
upon the dead coral of his own whims
sailing to the place that no longer exists
with a heavy ballast of whisky and gin
he cannot chart for tomorrow
today is beyond his means;
a cartographer to a setting red sun
a privateer of sunken old dreams

HEAVY OUT

There's not much for me to say
and there's even less that I can do
I can't heal those self-inflicted wounds
or unbind the chains of being you

But I'm here beside you, baby
and I'll walk along with you
no, I don't have the healer's touch
but I'm here to get you through

So each breath is a heavy in
and then there's that heavy out
just a repetition and a rhythm
when you're feeling all drawn out

You can't believe in anything,
but you can put your faith in me
I won't tell you that it's all easy
there's no cure for misery

I'm here beside you, baby
I'll try to see you through
I don't have that much to offer
but I'm always here for you
84

And each breath is a heavy in
then there's that heavy out
feel the breath of life within you
a succour from pain and doubt

HWY QE2

Oil stains, skid marks, and lost shoes

these are the landmarks of the prairies

a sign for Amish furniture

and the smell of cow piss

one hundred and ten kilometres an hour

and the scenery never changes

time and distance endless

insects pound the windshield

like fat drops of rain

a cereal grain desert

with mustard coloured patches

of canola and roadside turnouts

long-deserted gas stations

and decaying timber posts

crooked like hobo teeth

poking up through wild grass

and slutty culverts

but the road hums

and the skies are blue and wide

Chapter V:

Love, Hate, and Indifference

A VALKYRIE'S TEARS

I came home late one evening
I had been cruel and so unkind
she was tired of all my suffering
I was drunk and nearly blind

In the morning she made coffee
as the sun began to rise
the light was white and so unyielding
to these desperate pleading eyes

My hands were dry and trembling
and she said that 'it's alright'
I thought that she'd be vengeful
she took my hand and held it tight

We made love later that evening
while the moon caressed the sky
her perfumed hair fell across her bosom
while sadness fell from loving eyes

And I saw her from my darkness,
this goddess, bathed in purest light
I never thought she would forgive me
yet I felt redemption within her sight

88

If I had known it would be the last time
I would have begged, I would have lied
I would have offered up this ragged soul
just to be a shadow at her side

And now the days are soulless
I often think of her and I;
how she rose above my madness
that night I made an angel cry

LOVE HERETICAL

I don't know why I left you

in those days of used to be

maybe I loved you just a little bit less

than how much I loved me

that's how it always goes you know

we love as much as we can

and it's always just a little bit less

than ourselves, you understand?

You can never truly love another

but you can love the way that it feels

it's the guilty pleasures that I respect,

no more pretending, let's get real

I'm not into the personal spaces

those gaps between yourself and me

we both come first, you know it's true,

there's no crime in this heresy

What is love, when you break it all down,

is it the void in our souls revealed?

if that is the inspiration of god itself

does worship still hold its appeal?

when does all of the selfishness end

after the smiles run wet with pain,

when laughter grows distant, and silence is kept

or when the need is all that remains?

I'm not saying the poison is bitter

it's as sweet as the devil can make

never go begging on old lovers beds

they know you're on the take

it's all about you, it's all about me,

and it's all about everyone else

poets are always to blame, we say

we're so good at revealing ourselves

CONFLUENCE

It's dangerous and murky
where the river meets the sea
the churn of brackish waters
in the confluence of 'used to be'

Blended colours in this painting
the portrait of you and me
all mingled in the mixture
of our joy and misery

Where mistrust and understanding
are both the methods and the means
in that parabola of wisdom
that encompasses all we see

I hope you find fulfillment
or maybe, just the seeds
I pray you find your 'ever-after'
and that it's well received

I can promise you an ending
and I will most gratefully concede
you won't need a prophet
to separate our seas

TRANSACTION COMPLETE

Your love is a transaction

a note that you

brought back to me

I never thought it was tender

but I thought

that it was free

The tenderness you gave

went well with the kisses

that you wore

is our fashion so out of date?

are you are needing

something more?

Take this credit to the bank

but you cannot

cash it in

all the laughter

that we drank

all the lies that kept us thin

The line of credit has expired

there is no collateral

that you can place

the standard long abandoned

by any measure

of the state

LIPSTICK

I can't think

when she distracts me

like that

the lipstick she wore

left impressions

on the glass

where her

lips touched

while she

swallowed

every last drop

I can still taste

the wine;

fruity with notes

of oak and pear

her perfume scented

leather gloves

the ones she left

on the kitchen table

last night

before she went

home to her

husband

DIVIDED LANES

tall grass wilts

with lingering regrets

ambering beneath

a lemon sun

cars buzz on

like angry wasps

against the wind

a background

of chattering locust legs

click in clattering song

while asphalt heat shimmers

against a clear blue sky

she's late again

leaning against

the trunk of an old beater

he takes off his hat

wipes his brow

rubs his weathered neck

kicks at loose pebbles

scuffing them over

the roadside shoulder

96

they fall like rain

over a corrugated culvert

that coughs of dust

dead cattails sigh

in a choir of yesterdays

days that were meant

to be different

THERE WAS A LIGHT

THERE WAS A LIGHT

There was a light

from on above

illumination bright, white-hot

like the goddess love

it passed away

in a wink of time

I could not say how long it was

she was never really mine

I had been blind

I could not see

though it shone right through

every single part of me

Now I am lost

bereft of time

banished to the shadows

where the aching heart resigns

I carry on

the memory shrouds

though I know I never ever said

your sacred prayers aloud

I have grown cold,

I am living proof
what once was, now lost
the conclusion resolute
though I fought long
to find this truth
there is no way past
the sweet consoling lie of youth

I cannot die
you call to me
I will chart my final course
by the only light I see
I am consumed
consigned to be
a river that is swallowed
by a thirsting sea

There was a light
from on above
illumination bright, white-hot,
like the goddess love

WHEN YOU THINK OF US

Has enough time passed

for us to laugh again?

does the bitter pill

still stick in your dry throat?

has the liquor mellowed

and smoothed with age or does

it bite with unceremonious venom?

I see you there, across the table

your arms folded across your chest

shielded Roman sentries

with golden eagle crests

that do not move or fly

nostalgia for another time

perhaps, when your hair has greyed

your breasts have sagged

your skin thinned like rolled parchment

when your face is worn with the trail

of countless travels

maybe then

when you look upon the journey

and sigh softly

closing your eyes for the last time

will you smile

when you think of us

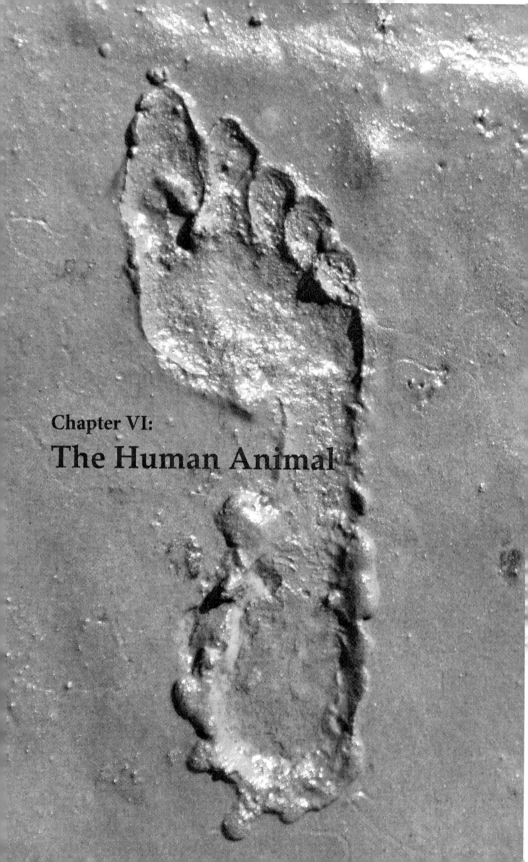

Chapter VI:
The Human Animal

OLD BARK

There's another spot

on my forearm

raised and brownish

I hadn't noticed it before

I suppose nobody has

a few new blemishes

skin tags popping

like buds in spring

an undiscovered country

of fresh real estate

I'm growing

they say a man should grow

I've got unexpected hair in places too

it's not like puberty

the novelty of becoming a man

not like that at all

more like a withering

fading into the background

where you go unnoticed

like black and white pictures

covering walls in restaurants

curiosity at a passing glance

you don't care about the story

or the miles

not really

you might find yellowed letters

in an old desk

that reeks of blue ink and age

 it's all going out

in the yard sale

or maybe the dump

if nobody wants it

after the winter ends

in the spring

GARDEN

She knelt in the garden

a watering can beside her

plucking deadheads

from the flowers

that she grew

tucking them into her apron

she brushed her hands

of the dirt

and gently watered the plants

new faces would rise again

and smile for a while

in the warm sun

before the wilting displeasure

claimed them too

CHAMPAGNE AGAIN

What brings you

to the corridors of the past?

was it something familiar?

do you come here often?

I've been known to roam the halls

looking for an ice machine

to fill my champagne bucket

I see a lot of wing-backed chairs

and glass ashtrays

teak end tables and synthetic plants

I pass so many numbered doors

I hear the voices, moans, and laughter

mingling in incoherent mutters

I think that I've forgotten

which room was mine

and can't help wondering

if I will ever taste

champagne again

EATING CHICKEN

EATING CHICKEN

He stood there

eating chicken over the kitchen sink

he was a second-rate man

draped by his own sagging flesh

the master of a tired domain

and the peculiar owner

of a singular solitude

a wretched slave to ambivalence

looking solemnly through

his aluminum framed window

watching his neighbour wash dishes

she's not young, but middle aged

handsome in a classic way

he imagined that she was lonely

and that the only warmth

she ever got was from

her soapy dishes

BOOTS

Coffee black mud
rich in the company
of bleached
crustacean shells
slick kelp whips
and flickering sea lice
a rubber boot
remains entrenched
a stumble
of prophetic curses
leads to the parliament
of quack grass
and the security
of lethargic hills
the tide will be in soon;
the sentinel drowned
beneath salt water flows
unresolved, a mystery remains
elsewhere, a meaning lost

THE CURSE OF CHURCHILL SQUARE

He had a battery powered amp
and a microphone set to bleed
barking out to strangers
to convey his desperate creed
a praise unto to the Lord!
a command for all to heed!

What happened to his reason
to make this seem alright?
was it the drugs or just conviction
that led him to this plight?
people kept on passing
and they kept expressions tight

Accusations out to all!
as they avoid his hateful glance
his wide and vacant eyes
delusional and entranced
he's been screeching there for hours
erect with rigid stance

The police were called to see him
he was asked to tone it down

he pointed to street performers
and the buskers all around
"God commands my very being,
His voice will not be drowned!"

Described, at best, "annoying"
by the patrons of the square
his voice was hardly music
to anyone who travelled there
but how to shut that noise up?
"Free speech!" he would declare

That is where the story ends
he's still loud beyond compare
megaphones and amplifiers
and that wild unhinged stare
we'd love to see him leave
he's still screaming over there!

There is a price for freedom
as my eardrums are aware
I go at length to avoid that place
that they call, "Churchill Square"
perhaps, he will move on one day
I'd look, but I don't dare.

He had a battery powered amp

and a microphone set to bleed,

barking out to strangers

to convey his desperate creed

a praise unto to the Lord!

a command for all to heed!

DINER

The middle aged man
sat at a table for two
crumbling his plastic wrapped saltines
dropping the broken crumbs
into the cold soup
he had been nursing
for half an hour
he sipped at lukewarm water
kept his head down
he opened a book that sat
on the table beside him
returning to the same
dog-eared page
he had turned to
so many times before
there was nothing special
on that page
he had read the first
few sentences before
but never seemed to get past
that opening paragraph

PEPPER MILL

His neck cracked

like a pepper mill

a canyon grimace

meandered

through the desert

carved by crowfoot

memories

long since flown

past on

tumbleweed dust

to a backdrop

of painted mountains

and pastel skies

VANITY

He combed his hair

while looking

in the bathroom mirror

realizing

as he groomed himself

that none of this could change

how old he had become

the fun pizzazz,

that little spark

that danced in the corners

of the eyes of the living

had not winked out

but faded

chuckling to himself

he put the hairbrush

back down

on the chipped

laminate vanity top

and clicked out

the light

Chapter VII:
Endings and Farewells

LET'S DO FEAR

LET'S DO FEAR

Let's do fear
together baby
I'll be weak
and you'll be strong

Our supplicated
screaming
such a sweet
angelic song

We'll bathe simply
in the gleaning
we may do right
we may do wrong

But can't we live
to split the difference
tip the scale
and move along?

116

FAMILIAR

You have to stop

the numbing;

the narcotics

the alcohol

and just live

in your own miseries

get to know them

like welcome old friends

extend shaking hands

in nicotine stained greetings

and toothless smiles

sit down

on some rickety

wooden chairs

across a beaten

kitchen table

light up fat cigars

put your feet up

share some stories

and when you finally reach

that level of intimacy

and truly know one another

then it's time;

time to drink

drink until you forget

that you ever

knew any of them

at all

HUNGER ARTIST

I know that you did your best
that you tried so much to care
the sweetest lies and tired passions
your wooden touch and nylon hair
I don't blame you for being hollow
I consumed everything you gave
I know there's nothing left of you
you're a hunger artist in a cage
I didn't mean to trap you there
your performance so neatly staged
the audience that came and went
fleeting interests are all the rage
I hear that there's another circus
where you can wither your life away
another butcher to eat your dying love,
your heart, and all of you that remains

DETAILS

You see it in his eyes

in the dull cataracts left behind

when spirits withdrew

like winter shadows

in greyscale landscapes

you see it in his walk

and in the way clothing hangs

like wet laundry

soaked shoulders slumping

dripping heavy with weight

you see it when he smiles

and looks pleased to see you

he's never been better

maybe he tells you

a self-deprecating joke

a hangman's grin

beneath a stitched hood

you see it in every detail

when you stand there

before the mirror

brushing your teeth

PLATITUDES

I've given you my platitudes
and a bandage for your wrists
that's all I've got
it isn't much
I've got nothing more than this

I know that may be troubling
after everything you've done
you did your best
you fought the war
some battles can't be won

I've been a professional loser
for more than half my life
I didn't mean
to drag you down
I know it wasn't right

I was desperate, I was selfish
I didn't know it at the time
I didn't mean
to kill your love
am I still guilty of the crime?

You call out for compassion

you've taken all of mine

you've done it before

you'll do it again

my empathy has resigned

You say you need me now

but it's more than I can give

I tried my best

I really did

but that's no way to live

PRISONER

The prisoner lies before you

his hand and feet in chains

no guards are there to keep him

yet in the prison he remains

you try your best to free him

with your compassion and your skill

but the prison is the spirit

the chains are his free will

There is no point in trying,

There is no rapture for this state...

You can reach out there to touch him

he doesn't feel a trace

you feel betrayal like bloody treason

because he draws you to this place

you will offer him temptation

you can plead and you can cry

you've offered your salvation

the bastard just won't try

There is no angelic choir playing,

There is no saving grace...

And he stares into the distance
like you haven't done a thing
you glance far into this future
and take off this diamond ring
if you linger here much longer
you will have to find a place
in the prison there, beside him,
imprisoned by disgrace

There are no answers left,
Salvation lies in your escape…

EQUATIONS

You can't help
a desperate man
while he's still making pleas
you can't put an end to suffering
to someone on their knees

You can't offer
any reasons
to a presence that isn't there
you can't bring salvation to
a man consumed by cares

The wondering
ain't all that easy
when the reasons just aren't there
there's no compassion to understanding
sometimes there's nothing fair

Time and distance
will always draw you
to a place without despair
after you lose that last connection
to a love no longer there

I SAW WHERE YOU WERE GOING

A ragged tangle of flesh
threw itself outside a window
like an accident
like a silence

no more dreaming, no more anger,
no more fear

A ragged tangle of flesh
cracks across the pavement
bits of glass
scrapes of dirt

no more pleading, no more love,
no more pain

A ragged tangle of flesh
bagged inside a cooler
a manila folder
a made up name

no more addiction, no more laughs,
no more tears

126

Oh, ragged tangle of flesh

I saw where you were going

Chapter VIII:
Fais Ton Nom

EPITAPH FOR BAZOOKA JOE

Juke box country

scratches stifled speakers

irritating the sore throat

of an overcast Monday morning

early coffee drips for the grey sunrise

you can't see the sun

it cries locked behind the clouds

but you know it's there

it's a matter of scientific faith

sweeping sidewalk pebbles fall

to dark asphalt waves

that rise and roll

like tired ripples

from a stone cast

on a placid lake

the door chimes

a cheap synthetic tone

but it's Mozart to my ears

rising above the affected twang

of another Styrofoam song

like every other you hear

pre-wrapped and packaged

deep down

in my dusty jean pocket

I find Bazooka Joe

he's pink, hard, and stale

covered in powdered sugar

awful and saccharine

but he comes with a cartoon

it has more words

than a volume of modern poetry

you can roll your eyes

in response

maybe laugh a little

before tossing it to the trash

a fitting epitaph

for popular culture

FAME

FAME

Lost forever

in a moment

a little glimpse

and then it's gone

a lost but gentle gleaning

the last refrain

of final song

Another glimpse

another moment

before the breaking

of the dawn

a fretful-smile and tearful parting

the soft farewell

of moving on

As a disciple

of long foreboding

the fatal silence

that fills all sound

the eternal fleeting moment

ends a time

once thought profound

JOB

I have prayed to succeed
to avoid the crushing failure
so blessed by the Lord
I am punished
by His favour

I am beaten to submission
though I do not know my crime
humiliated by the grace
and the passing
of my time

Confined to a selfish prison
by shackles I am defined
compelled to scribe each verse
with no audience
left in mind

Another failing soul cries out
whispers on the wind
hymns cast up to heaven
will they ever
let them in?

But my faith

it never waivers

it never fails to entreat

so pious and so penitent

posthumous and complete

LOVE AND INDIFFERENCE

And now it's time
for this final phrase
there are no longer starlit nights
and there are no more dancing days
but time keeps moving on
it's not delayed;
it's cruel and it's relentless
and so heartless in decay

I saw your footprints
melting in the snow
it's been a while, I ask myself
why did you have to go?
and although you told me
time again, I still don't know
tell me once more and maybe
your breath can kiss me while it blows

Now it's half my fault
I might be willing to concede
if I've only thought of myself
it's because I'm so very full of need

but I want you here
beside me in my greed
your ebbing love and indifference
is the shoreline to my sea

I'm standing here alone
upon this aging stage
I'm stringing up an effigy
built for a pyre of my disgrace
the crowd here is ambivalent;
ghosts haunt their favorite place
I can't see you from the spotlight
I'm so blinded by your grace

MADE

A visage carved in marble
a hero kept from age
the great performance
of an actor
while a man lies in the grave

I'm picking out the costume
and the make-up
I should wear
that picture in the newspaper
that 'persona au contraire'

It isn't for the theatre
the limelight, or the stage
the deconstruction of
this character
is a war that's always waged

To reveal all the secrets
that lurk beneath one's skin
components disassembled
recombined
made whole again

I prefer a little distance
from the faces I have played
but I want you all to love me
at least, this person
I have made

STRAIGHT LINE

There's a hate that calls me in
like a sinner to the sin;
the boutique perfume
of a dying rose

There's a sadness that it brings
a lonely pyre of offerings
left there by the wretched
and the meek

The sweet hug a drink can wring
you're a lone and desperate thing
smiles that fall in-between
the ruins and the rains

A drink to you, my favourite friend
I never lie, I just pretend;
a street mime walking
a straight line against the wind

WANNABE COWBOY POET

WANNABE COWBOY POET

I always wanted to write poetry

about some storied place

like Texas, in a dusty roadside cantina

where life is lived cheap and wild

and there's a big-titted barmaid

who says something hip and profound

in the context of an old boot

and a caked on mascara wink

where the dust and scuff marks

on the weathered hardwood floor

could tell you more about life

and the universe

than a philosophy major

tripping on acid or cactus juice

it seems the good shit

is always going on somewhere else

and to someone else

somewhere I've never been

or someplace I'm unlikely to go

given my frail constitution

I'm not much of a hero these days

or any other day

driving my cheap desk

to the dusty horizon

of a setting golden sun

as with anywhere and all things

it's half lie and half truth

and it's not a place so much

I want to write about, but a time

everyone needs a goddamn hero

but the last one died

beside an ink-clacking typewriter

pounding on his nicotine stained keys

and broken old soul

EVOLUTION

I saw you writhing

with knuckle-clubbed fins

through the thick muck

of primordial ignorance

fish-lipped and fat

bloated and green

your gaping maw spills out

gurgling bubbles

of slimy, stagnant air

blubbering and bloated

gibbering gibberish

smiling with slick-smug satisfaction

they say that it takes

ten thousand hours

to become an expert;

your ten minute investment

means nothing

WAVES

the

chatter rolls

in gentle waves

subliminal smatterings

against smooth rocks

receding toward

the wetness

of a supple

tongue

licking out

occasional syllables

only half heard and then

drowned in gurgling

mumbles

a once

submissive

voice rises to the tide

a crescendo of meaning

crashes against rough stone

before receding slowly

softly back into

the cold

calm

WORMWOOD

He sat upon that park bench there
companions of insects in his hair
and cares that only dwelled
beneath his skin

He tried to find his place in time
for misfit thoughts and misfit rhymes
to cast aside a life of spreadsheet
dollar dreams

A poet pending in his mind
his temperance lost to modern crimes
he found the courage of
public self-defeat

From a holy book of calloused proofs
from painful places he spoke of truths
absconded by narcissists
and faux-bohemian thieves

His words still taunt him now and then
they chide to him in haunting hymns
muttering alone and to the ones
that consume His living flesh

144

There, his body and his blood,
stolen by those who cannot love
consumed and relished
with savoury parasitic grins

He once sat upon that park bench there
companions of insects in his hair
and cares that only dwelled
beneath his skin

GROPING FOR WORDS

Groping for words like a lover
nervous fumbling in the night
silence gasps in misunderstanding
syllables hidden in plain sight

He remembers all that he means
he can picture it all in his head
he 'ums' to fill awkward silence
the breath of each pause falls dead

He wonders and he's confounded
his family offers up nervous smiles
strangled by his own mutterings
he forgets every once in a while

I can see it upon my father
I am afraid as it begins in me
my words, my thoughts, my musings
lost to silence and misery

I'm not asking for some sympathy
I'm not asking God for His grace
I scramble to jot down the moments
before they are lost, forgotten, misplaced

DROWNING IN THE HALL

I'd like to thank you all for coming

maybe once or maybe twice

if you didn't get my meaning

I took my chance, I rolled the dice

and maybe that means nothing

when you're doing what you love

I'll stand before the tallest giants

while they shade me from above

their passions bleed all over me;

I fear I won't be heard at all

I'm painted by the same brush strokes

of every voice who's heard the call

About the Author

Christopher Raine was born in Halifax, Nova Scotia, Canada in 1968. He attended the University of Calgary and the University of Alberta where he studied English and Fine Art. He later studied Architectural Technology at Digital School in Edmonton, Alberta. In addition to his published materials, Raine has written and run creative writing workshops for the Morinville Community Public Library.

Also by Christopher Raine

Vacant Morality: Poems of the Past

ISBN-10: 1483478084

ISBN-13: 978-1483478081

Desperate and passionate, the poetry of Vacant Morality rolls off of the tongue like music. There are moments of simple purity filtered through the lens of experience, regret, and wisdom. Poet Christopher Raine believes the best way to explain beauty is through the contrast of ugliness. It is only through suffering that one can truly feel the unique rarity of sublime love and hope. The dark nature of this poetry collection is insightful and deeply reflective, whether it is the political vigilance of "The Abattoir," the condemnation of "The Hallowed," or the soulful longing of "You Want:" The work is underscored with themes of social justice, shared through a no-nonsense style that feels cool and smooth in its cadence and vibe. Readers will appreciate Raine's thoughtful, passionate treatment of subjects familiar to many.

www.RaineReflections.com